5

Are We Having Fun Yet?

75 Ways to Create a
Motivating Work Environment

Regina M. Clark, CSP

ISBN 978-0-615-28080-6
Library of Congress Control Number: 2009903208

Published and distributed by
Clark Training and Development
PO Box 383, Goshen, NY 10924

Tel: 845-294-7089
Fax: 845-294-6783
www.AreWeHavingFunYetBook.com

Cover design by Marc Tolen, Creative Graphics, www.cgmt.com

Interior design by Jill Ronsley, SUN Editing & Book Design, www.suneditwrite.com

Printed and bound in the USA

Acknowledgment

This book is dedicated to the thousands of people in my audiences who have made me laugh.

Contents

Introduction

HOW TO MOTIVATE EMPLOYEES has always been a difficult question. On the one hand, we can say that it's not possible to motivate employees at all—people typically do what they want to do. They are motivated by their own reasons, not by yours. On the other hand, research has proven that there is a strong relationship between happy employees and productivity.

If all we really know about employee motivation is that it is not an exact science, how do we ensure that our employees are happy and motivated? One thing that employers can do is to create an environment or corporate culture that is motivating. This book is full of suggestions collected from a wide variety of employers. Many of the ideas come straight from my audiences. As I traveled the country and spoke about having fun at work, people told me what they were doing at their company that was special. The ideas come from large global organizations and from mom-and-pop businesses; some of them are simple to implement, while others take strategic planning and a budget. As you read through the ideas, keep in mind that every organization and every employee is different. What works at Google might not work at Smith Barney. What motivates a 45-year-old mother of three might not work for a 23-year-old single male. What works in Newark, New Jersey might not work in Hong Kong. What works for civil service employees might not work for entrepreneurs. Experiencing fun at work is an individual thing.

Your challenge as an employer is to create a fun, motivating environment for all your employees—the Baby Boomers born between 1946 and 1964, the Generation X employees born between

1965 and 1976, and the Generation Y employees born between 1977 and 2002. You also have to keep in mind that you are dealing with a diverse workforce. Employees come in all colors, sizes and shapes. They speak a variety of languages and bring diverse experiences to the workforce. Finally, we are going through one of the worst recessions since the Great Depression. Unemployment is at an all-time high, the stock market has taken a beating and many employees are fearful that they will lose their jobs. Employers are challenged to do more with less. I can't think of a better time to create a motivating work environment.

What, exactly, is fun?

IF I ASKED ONE HUNDRED PEOPLE to tell me what "fun" means, I would probably get one hundred different answers. When we think of fun, most of us think of having fun, experiencing fun or participating in a fun event or an enjoyable activity. Every year, I watch in amazement as thousands of people crowd Times Square in New York City to watch the ball drop on New Year's Eve. I'm sure the people who are there would tell you that they are having fun, but you couldn't pay me to go to Times Square on New Year's Eve. The crowds are massive, the temperature is usually below freezing, and the hotel rooms are wildly expensive; unless you have a VIP pass you are not going to get near the stage, you can't bring alcohol, and there is really not that much to see—it only takes the crystal ball a few seconds to drop. My idea of an enjoyable New Year's Eve would be to sit in front of the fire with my husband and a good bottle of wine. Has my idea of fun changed as I've aged? You bet it has!

Did you know that FUN is also the acronym for the Faculty of Undergraduate Neuroscience? That is an international organization focused on undergraduate neuroscience education and research. I don't know about you, but teaching neuroscience doesn't sound like fun to me—although I'm sure that the people who teach neuroscience do enjoy teaching it. They might even have fun in their classrooms.

According to *Merriam-Webster's Dictionary*, "fun" means "something that provides amusement or enjoyment." Fun can also be used as an adjective to describe a person; for example, "a fun guy," also known as Steve Martin. When we add "ny" to fun, we end up with "funny," which is all about laughing. Steve Martin definitely makes us laugh!

The challenge in creating fun at work is that everyone has a different idea of what fun is. I love what I do for a living. I have fun speaking to audiences, meeting new people, traveling to new places and coaching others. Yet I know lots of people who would not enjoy doing what I do for a living. The thought of having to get up in front of 1,500 people and speak to them would make them physically ill. The thought of traveling to a foreign country alone would make them anxious, and the thought of coaching another person would put them over the edge. We all have to figure out what we enjoy doing for a living and then go do it. For a variety of reasons, that's not always as easy as it sounds. Sometimes people don't know what they like to do, or they are too scared to do what they dream of doing, or their life circumstances don't allow them to find a job that they love, or they don't have the proper education to do what they want to do. With so many people losing their jobs lately, people are becoming less selective about what they do for a living as long as they are earning a paycheck. The country music singer David Allen Coe even wrote a song called "Take this Job and Shove It," about the bitterness of a man who worked long and hard with no apparent reward. In 1981, "Take this Job and Shove It" became a movie. The reality is that not everyone likes his or her job. As employers, we can figure out ways for employees to hate their jobs a little bit less. If you are not sure whether or not you really like your job, ask yourself this question: If you won the lottery tomorrow, would you show up for work?

My husband is a veteran New York City Police officer. He works in a drug-infested, high-crime precinct in northern Manhattan. When he started working there, the precinct was a dangerous place with one of the highest crime ratings in New York City. It would be a real stretch to say that he has fun at work. Once in a while, he might get to see something or do something fun that most people wouldn't get to do (like standing in front of the stage at a Rod Stewart concert, or working the finish line at the NYC Marathon, or meeting Harrison Ford, or watching a Yankee game from the dugout), but for the most part his days are full of handling domestic disputes, dealing with drunks and drug dealers, arresting criminals, communicating with condescending District Attorneys and doing paperwork. So, you might ask, can the New York City Police Department create a motivating work environment? Of course they can! They can treat people fairly, give credit where it's due, provide quality training, uniforms and equipment for their officers, offer great benefits and fair compensation and treat officers with kindness, respect and a sense of humor.

Many police officers, firemen and other civil servants are motivated by the great benefits package they receive and the camaraderie they experience. After twenty years of active duty, New York City Police officers and firefighters can retire and collect a pension for the rest of their lives. Today, being able to collect a pension is a real benefit. Most employers don't provide pensions.

We may not be able to say definitively what fun at work is, but we can say what it's not.

Fun at work is not:

- teasing or ridiculing others
- playing harmful practical jokes on people
- discriminating on the basis of sexual orientation, religion, gender, race or anything else
- being mean
- treating people disrespectfully
- creating unsafe working conditions
- putting employees in situations they can't handle
- withholding compensation

Fun at work is—well, that's what the suggestions that follow will help you find out.

1. Ask employees their opinions and listen to what they say.

In 2005, the University of Michigan created a Web site called VOICES (www.voices.umich.edu), which allows a staff of more than 25,000 to voice their concerns, suggestions, ideas and comments on a wide variety of issues. About one hundred staff members from all areas of the University community were selected to become the initial VOICES team. A subset of that group has a direct dialogue with the University's executive officers and shares ideas regularly with the University's President and Associate Vice President for Human Resources. VOICES is one of the reasons *The Chronicle of Higher Education* identified the University of Michigan as one of the best universities to work for.

Greg Johnson, senior director of Process Solutions at Medtronic, in Fridley, Minnesota asks his employees to put marbles in a jar to measure how their work is impacting the company's overall business strategy. Every week, employees put different-colored marbles in a jar. Red marbles signify a disconnect with work and corporate strategy, blue marbles signify the normal status quo and green marbles signify that great work is occurring. At the end of the month, the marble jar is discussed in the monthly staff meeting. So far, employees have responded favorably to the marble jar. It's a bit goofy and silly, but it does open up lines of communication between employees and supervisors.

Eagles Talent Connection Inc., a small employer in New Jersey, strives to make all its employees feel equal by asking for their opinions on any new idea or project that is implemented, be it redoing the Web site or revising a marketing flyer. Everyone in the office has a stake in the outcome of all that is accomplished.

When you provide employees with a mechanism for sending messages, such as a suggestion box, you must make sure that you also provide a mechanism for responding to the messages. Listening to employees and acknowledging their ideas and input without retribution is essential to creating a motivating work environment.

2. Treat every employee as a valued asset.

Abraham Lincoln once began a letter by saying, "Everybody likes a compliment." Everyone wants to be appreciated. Many organizations have formal and informal reward and recognition programs. Most people appreciate it when their employer or supervisor takes the time to thank them for a job well done. A thank-you could come in the form of a verbal announcement, a write-up in the company newsletter, a handwritten note, a gift certificate for a pint of Ben & Jerry's ice cream or a fully paid trip to Australia. There are so many outstanding ways to reward and recognize employees!

At the New York Air National Guard base in Orange County, New York, medals are awarded for good deeds and achievements. These medals are presented at mass formation, where a citation is read and the medal is pinned on the recipient's uniform.

At Crystal Run Healthcare in Orange County, New York, employees are nominated to receive stars. Anyone can nominate someone else for a star. The nominee gets an e-mail with an attachment; when the attachment is opened, a big star explodes on the nominee's desktop with a message from the person who nominated him or her. The employees save up their stars and trade them in for gift certificates to local vendors.

The Bardavon Opera House, which is the oldest continuously operating theater in New York State, has a "twinkling star" recognition program. The star is passed from employee to employee, based on the previous week's activities. This accomplishes several things: it rewards employees for good work (the star is displayed on the employee's office door for the week), it causes the holder to consider the performance of his or her peers, and it helps polish public speaking skills, since the holder must explain his reasons for choosing the person to whom the star is passed.

If you are looking for more ideas on how to reward and recognize employees, read *1001 Ways to Reward Employees* by Bob Nelson, or *The Carrot Principle* by Gostick and Elton. Both books share formal and informal was to recognize individuals and teams.

3. Keep the work environment clean.

Bright, tidy and organized beats dirty, dingy and chaotic any day of the week. Every retailer will tell you that maintaining a clean and organized store environment is part of his customer service strategy. Your employees are your internal customers. They want to come to work and not be disgusted by having to use a dirty restroom or broken-down equipment. Maintaining a tidy workplace also sets the trend for employee behavior. If management or owners don't care enough to keep their business in good order, why should their employees care?

Many employers schedule "clean out your office" days. During these events, employees are encouraged to come to work in work clothes, get rid of junk that has accumulated in offices and storage spaces and recover recyclable and reusable materials. Cleaning and reorganizing is more fun and efficient if many people participate. An organized clean-out frees up storage space in addition to recycling idle papers that may be cluttering up the files.

4. Form a Green Team to improve your work environment and the environment in which you live.

Putting together a Green Team at work will raise employee awareness of opportunities to save energy and contribute to a healthy work environment. The Green Team can work together to suggest ways to be eco-friendly at work. The Green Team should be a cross-functional team and have key stakeholders on board. It would be wise to include people from purchasing and communications on the team.

Studies have shown that being eco-friendly eventually adds money to the bottom line. Here are a few suggestions:

- Make recyclable bins available.
- Use energy-efficient lighting.
- Convert general lighting to task lighting.

17

- Minimize paper.
- Address indoor air quality and noise.
- Replace toxic cleaning products with least-toxic alternatives.

5. Promote safety

As an employer, you have the responsibility of providing a safe work environment for all employees, one that is free from any hazards and complies with all state and federal laws. Health and safety in the workplace means preventing work-related injury and disease, and designing an environment that promotes the well-being of everyone at work. The Occupational Safety and Health Act states that every working American has the right to a safe and healthy work environment. The Occupational Safety and Health Administration (OSHA) is the federal agency created to enforce the Occupational Safety and Health Act.

Knowledge is the key ingredient in providing a safe work environment. If everyone knows the correct procedures, accidents and injuries can be kept to a minimum. Every employer should develop and have in place an occupational health and safety policy that meets the following standards:

- Ensure that the way work is done is safe and does not affect employees' health.
- Ensure that tools, equipment and machinery are safe and are kept safe.
- Ensure that ways of storing, transporting or working with dangerous substances are safe and do not damage employees' health.
- Provide employees with the information, instruction and training they need to do their jobs safely and without damaging their health.
- Consult with employees about health and safety in the workplace.
- Monitor the workplace regularly and keep a record of what is found during the checks.

Safety and safety training are serious subjects. Just ask the 155 passengers aboard the US Airways Flight 1549 that landed safely in the Hudson River on January 13, 2009. Those passengers owe their lives to the experienced, properly trained crew led by Captain Chesley B. Sullenberger III. The crew and rescuers did what they were trained to do, and they did it quickly. They did not have to stop and check the safety manual. They responded the way they were trained.

There are many simple, easy ways to promote safety in the workplace. Garbage should never be stored in inappropriate areas or block emergency exits. Many employers, both large and small, have been fined for blocking emergency exits and not following OSHA-mandated safety procedures. In 1991, 25 workers died in a North Carolina poultry-processing plant in which the fire exits were blocked, locked or inadequately marked.

Employers should also provide comfortable desk chairs to reduce repetitive movement injuries and back pain, and proper lighting to reduce eye strain.

Timely snow removal is another part of keeping the work environment safe. You don't want your employees to slip and fall on ice as they are walking into the building.

For more information about safety in the workplace, go to www.osha.gov.

6. Smile!

If you see someone without a smile on his face, give him one of yours.

Carol King once wrote, "You've got to get up every morning with a smile on your face and show the world all the love in your heart. Then people are gonna treat you better...." It's true. People do treat you better when you smile at them. Your smile communicates volumes. It tells people, "I like you. I'm happy to be with you. I'm enjoying your company. I'm glad we are working together. I'm having a good day." When you smile at people, they often smile back at you. Usually a smile communicates pleasure, amusement and happiness.

It's a lot easier to work with happy people than it is to work with grumpy, negative people. Most people are seeking happiness.

In his groundbreaking best-seller *How to Win Friends and Influence People,* Dale Carnegie wrote an entire chapter about the power of smiling. He shares the ancient Chinese proverb, "A man without a smiling face must not open a shop."

If you really want to have fun, buy some smiles on a stick and pass them out at work. Smiles on a stick are available from The HUMOR Project, www.thehumorproject.com. The HUMOR Project was started over twenty years ago by Dr. Joel Goodman to help people get more smileage out of their lives and jobs by applying the practical, positive power of humor and creativity.

7. Be friendly.

James D. Miles once said, "You can easily judge the character of a man by how he treats those who can do nothing for him."

Take the time to develop friendly relationships at work. Say hello to people every day, and use their names. It only takes a moment to say hello. We all know negative, grouchy people. Most of us don't want to work with these people. Negative people suck the energy out of us. Employees need you to build them up, not knock them down. Your job is to be a role model for positive, professional communication. Years ago, I worked with a senior vice president of operations at a large footwear company. Everyone loved him because he took the time to learn everyone's name and always said hello to people.

8. Encourage individual growth and development.

Provide resources and encouragement for employees to learn and grow. Tuition reimbursement, education bonuses for outstanding student loans, on-site training programs, external training programs, a lending library, teleseminars, webinars, mentoring and job rotations are all opportunities for employees at every level to learn new skills.

The launching of corporate universities is a growing trend for corporations. Denise Hearn, in her article "Education in the Workplace: An Examination of Corporate University Models," notes that in 1993 corporate universities existed in only 400 companies. Today, there are many more. Some of the American companies known for their training excellence include Motorola, Disney, Xerox, Intel, IBM, Medtronic and Corning. In 1993, as Manager of Management Development, I was responsible for launching the Meldisco Business Academy. Meldisco was a division of the Melville Corporation, which sold footwear in Kmart stores nationwide. The courses for the Meldisco Business Academy were taught by experts, training professionals and external consultants. We offered a wide variety of programs for all employees, from entry-level associates through senior executives; the subjects included Retail Math, Behavioral Interviewing, Doing Business in China, Merchandise Planning and Communicating on Camera. The programs were conducted live at the corporate office. Eventually, we partnered with IBM in Armonk, New York and used their state-of-the-art training facilities to broadcast the programs to remote locations.

Today, companies are using technology to keep the cost of corporate training down. Employees participate in webinars and teleseminars while at their desks. Some companies, such as Medtronic, offer courses via satellite. Every year, Medtronic publishes a course catalog for their employees. Some of the courses offered via satellite have included Excellence in Leadership and Management, taught by Dr. Ken Blanchard; Leadership and Emotional Intelligence, taught by Daniel Goleman; Execution, taught by Larry Bossidy, former Chairman and CEO of Honeywell International; and Organizational Transformation, taught by Louis Gerstner.

There is no limit to what you can offer your employees. Smart employees will take advantage of as much training and development as they can.

9. Have a succession plan.

The general definition of succession planning is the process of preparing to hand over control. Business succession planning is the process of preparing to hand over control of the business to others in a way that is least disruptive to the business's operations and value. Great companies take succession planning very seriously. They identify candidates early to move into key senior positions, and they offer development plans for these individuals. It's too bad that our government doesn't do succession planning; it would make the President much more effective when he is sworn into office.

In 1994, years before he retired from General Electric, Jack Welch started the succession planning process. He developed a list of the qualities, skills and characteristics that a CEO should have, so that GE was ready for its next CEO years before it finally made the decision in 1999. Three senior executives were identified as possible replacements for Jack: Jeff Immelt, James McNerney and Robert Nardelli. All three were experienced, knowledgeable and capable of doing the job. When GE finally announced that Jeff Immelt would take over as CEO, James McNerney was recruited by 3M to be their new CEO. The 3M stock rose 34 percent on his watch. In 2005, McNerney left 3M for Boeing. Robert Nardelli accepted a position with Home Depot as their CEO; he did not do so well there. He came under fire for the size of his pay package as well as his management style. Nardelli eventually stepped down as the CEO of Home Depot and left with a $210 million severance package. He is currently the CEO of Chrysler, one of Detroit's struggling automakers. Whether or not Nardelli will be able to turn Chrysler around is yet to be seen.

Having a succession plan in place smoothes the way for continued success in any business.

10. Encourage innovative thinking.

There are many ways to encourage innovate thinking. It's really up to you. Henry Ford once said, "If you think you can or if you think you can't, you're right." The first step to being an innovative thinker is to make a sincere commitment to innovation.

When was the last time you had a creative idea? Last week? Last month? A year ago? Are you stuck in your comfort zone? Do you embrace change or dread it? If you are not challenging the system on a daily basis, you will not move forward to achieve world-class results. To stay successful, businesses must develop new products and services, and they must find creative solutions to existing problems. Many highly educated, intelligent business executives know that fostering innovation is a smart thing to do, the right thing to do, the one thing that will set them apart from the competition—and still they fail to innovate. Why? Why do people and organizations fail to innovate even though they know they should? One reason could be because innovation is hard; it takes time, energy and sincere commitment. It's simply easier to keep doing things the way they have always been done. The problem with this is that if you keep doing things the same way, you keep getting the same results. And in the constantly changing world in which we live, the same results just don't cut it. Another reason that people resist being creative is because it isn't logical. It's easier to be a logical thinker than a creative thinker. It's easier to be an analytical thinker than a creative thinker. It's also safer to be a logical, analytical thinker than a creative thinker. Don't get me wrong—logic and analysis are important thinking skills. We use analytical skills to dig for the root cause of problems all the time. But we need creative skills to find creative solutions and innovative ideas.

Here are ten tips for encouraging innovative thinking. The tips are in no particular order, which may annoy some of you. Too bad! It's time to challenge the logical side of your brain.

Tip #1: Get rid of mental locks.

Did you ever hear someone say any of these lines?

- I'm not creative.
- Everything is fine the way it is.
- We've done all right so far.

- It's too much work.
- We don't have enough time to be creative.
- It's not my job.
- The staff will never buy it.
- We shouldn't be having this much fun at work.
- This stuff is silly.

These are all excuses. Get rid of the excuses!

Everyone is creative. We were each born with a brain that has two sides, a creative side and a logical, analytical side. We were all curious when we were little kids. We asked lots of questions and wondered about things. We asked the following questions:

- Why do birds fly?
- Why does water move?
- Why are monkey bars called monkey bars?
- What do foxes eat?
- Why do we have to color inside the lines?
- Why is the sun shaped like a bagel?
- How do kites fly?

Unfortunately, when we entered the school system, we were taught to think logically. We were told that there is only one right answer. We studied facts, and some of our creativity was squashed. Of course, as adults, we now know that there is often more than one right answer. Start asking "why" again. Challenge your thinking.

Tip #2: Use both sides of your brain.

Think of your brain as a muscle. When we use our muscles, the muscles become stronger. Wouldn't you love to have a stronger brain, enabling you to think better? You could read more efficiently, solve problems faster and improve your memory. Who knows what you are really capable of accomplishing?

Some people say that knowledge is power. Knowledge is powerful when it is used. There are knowledgeable people who don't do anything with their knowledge. Other knowledgeable people, who know a lot about a variety of things, have the creative ability to link random thoughts together to develop powerful ideas and solutions.

When was the last time you picked up a crayon, a marker or a paint set and drew a picture? When was the last time you sang out loud, danced the cha-cha, played a musical instrument or composed a song? How about using your digital camera to capture a bird in flight or a sunset? How about completing the *New York Times* crossword puzzle? I'm not talking about painting a masterpiece or singing on key; I'm just talking about developing the creative side of your brain. Do you allow yourself time each day to daydream? Do you ask yourself "what if" questions? In 1974, Tony Buzan wrote a book called *Use Both Sides of Your Brain*. It's about how the mind really works. We can develop thinking skills to use our brains more effectively.

Tip # 3: Learn creative thinking techniques and use them.

A variety of creative thinking techniques can be used to stimulate innovative thinking. You can learn some of these techniques by reading books or attending seminars. The simplest technique is brainstorming. Brainstorming is widely used and abused. When a group decides to brainstorm, they must follow brainstorming rules in order to be effective. Brainstorming must be timed. True brainstorming generates many ideas (quantity rather than quality), and no judging should be allowed. People need to be encouraged to build on each other's ideas. Often, participants analyze each other's ideas before the brainstorming is done. This ruins the brainstorming session. A good facilitator can put an end to the analysis quickly and get the brainstorming back on track.

Other techniques to promote creative thinking include the "Random Word Technique," "Creating Metaphors," "Thinking Like a Child," "The Six Thinking Hats," and "Mind Mapping." Books by Edward De Bono, Roger von Oech and Tony Buzan are full of such techniques. Many years ago, I watched Edward De Bono give a presentation to a large group of educators in which he showed them how to use creative thinking techniques to solve problems.

De Bono believes that our minds need to be provoked to think differently; that's why the "Random Word Technique" works so well. In this technique, you select a random word from a book or magazine, put that word on the top of a flipchart and start brainstorming. Anything that comes to anyone's mind goes on the flipchart. The words on the flipchart are then used to solve a real business problem.

Creative techniques are often introduced during process-improvement training. The participants select a particular technique and use it during an exercise. Unfortunately, however, most participants fail to apply the creative techniques outside the classroom. It's just easier not to.

Recently, I was working with a corporation's high-performance work team. We were doing an exercise on using innovative thinking, which is one of the organization's core values. The group decided that they were very creative. I asked them what techniques they used to stimulate creative thinking. Their response was, "What do you mean by techniques, we use brainstorming?" I said, "Did you ever try moving beyond brainstorming and trying other techniques like the 'Random Word Technique,' or 'Lateral Thinking,' or 'Think Like a Child,' or the 'Six Thinking Hats'?" The response was, "I guess we're not as creative as we could be." Using creative techniques can really help people jump start the creative thinking process.

Tip #4: Move outside your area of expertise.

Most of us hang around with people who are like us. We even hire people who are like us. At work, finance people have their own language, engineers work together, cops socialize with other cops, and senior executives have lunch with other senior executives. But different ideas come from people who think differently. Invite people from outside your area of expertise to join in your creative problem-solving. To stimulate your thinking, read magazines and journals that you don't regularly read. Learn about a variety of things, and see if you can make any connections to your own field. I read a story in *National Geographic Magazine* about John Smith. (I don't usually read *National Geographic*, my husband does.) John Smith enforced certain rules with the settlers in the New World, such as if they didn't work, they didn't eat. I used this example during a management training program to illustrate adult motivation: the settlers were clearly motivated to eat, so they worked.

Tip #5: Avoid the classic innovation traps.

In 2006, the *Harvard Business Review* published an article called "Innovation: The Classic Traps" by Rosabeth Moss Kanter. The article discussed case studies showing classic innovation traps that occur time and time again. For example, some companies fall into the trap of adopting a strategy of investing only in ideas that they think will become blockbusters; they ignore small ideas, which could generate big profit dollars. Other traps include process mistakes, structure mistakes and skills mistakes. The remedies include adding flexibility to planning, tightening the human connections between innovators and others in the organization and selecting innovation leaders with strong interpersonal skills, who know how to put teams together. If you are serious about implementing innovative practices in your organization, study the *Harvard Business Review* article.

Tip #6: Allow failures.

If you don't allow yourself to make mistakes, you will never learn from your mistakes. Innovative thinking is risky; the idea you generate might be the best idea ever or a total flop. Bad ideas can cost businesses money. When Coca-Cola introduced New Coke in April of 1985, they expected the new soft drink to replace Classic Coke. Instead, the launch of New Coke was a disaster. Public reaction was overwhelmingly negative. Consumers started to horde Classic Coke and sell it on the black market. By July, 1985, New Coke was pulled off the shelves. Recently, an energy drink called Cocaine was introduced by Redux Beverages, LLC. Naming a high-energy drink after an illegal drug is certainly risky business— creative, but risky! The FDA issued warnings that the drink was illegally marketed as a drug alternative and dietary supplement.

The beverage was pulled from the market, and the company plans to sell it under a new name.

Tip #7: Create a process map.

Before you can come up with creative solutions to a problem, you need to understand exactly what the problem is. To identify the problem, you must understand the work you do in terms of processes. Every process has a beginning and an end, with inputs and outputs. Years ago, the finance department of a corporation was trying to solve a payroll problem: workers were not getting paid on time, and the finance department was being blamed. Part of the problem was inaccurate or missing information; this information should have been collected by human resources during the initial hiring process. The finance department tried to fix the problem without including the human resource department in the solution. Finance blamed human resources and called them incompetent, but failed to include them when it came time to look for solutions. Developing a process map with a clearly defined beginning and end point helped this group solve their problem collaboratively.

Tip #8: Get people involved.

When it comes to stimulating creative ideas, the more people you are able to involve, the better. Include people from different areas with diverse knowledge and expertise, different backgrounds and different ages. The best way to find a good idea is to amass lots of ideas and then select the best one. Diverse teams will generate more creative ideas than homogeneous teams. Also, consider inviting external people to join your teams. External people have different points of view and no hidden agendas.

Tip #9: Get out of your own way.

We work our entire lives to develop skills and knowledge that serve us well. Sometimes we are so competent that we get in our own way. We think that because we have seen a certain situation before, we know the answer, or that we are prepared to solve a problem because we have the skills to do so. When I teach people how to facilitate participant-centered training, one of the most challenging things is to get subject-matter experts to shut up. These subject-matter experts have been selected to train other employees because they know the material and because they have effective presentation skills. In order to truly facilitate learning, however, good trainers must check their egos at the door. Good trainers know how to pull the answers out of the audience and how to check the understanding of the participants. After all, the focus of training isn't about the trainer; it's about getting the participants to learn. So get out of your own way, listen, and enter situations with an open mind.

Tip #10: Create an environment that supports innovative thinking.

When was the last time you took a trip to learn about something? Was it in grade school, or high school? Do you visit your competition? Do you purchase their products? Do you know what their work environment is like? Does your work environment stimulate innovative thinking? Do you have a suggestion program at work? Are books and other resources available? Do you use creative thinking techniques to stimulate your thinking? Are there opportunities to clear your head during the work day? Can you participate in developmental opportunities? According to *Fortune Magazine,* Google engineers are required to devote twenty percent of their time to pursuing projects they have dreamed up that will help the company. Google also provides its employees with lots of perks, such as rock-climbing walls, gourmet restaurants, and lap pools. Google recruits at Harvard, MIT and Stanford, looks for employees with diverse interests, hires smart people and works hard to keep its employees motivated. Google creates an environment where employees are stimulated to challenge their thinking.

11. Share information, business goals and strategic plans with the workforce.

The more employees know, the better they will perform. When employees know what their corporation's business goals are, there is a greater chance that they will work to achieve these goals. In his book *The 8th Habit*[1], Stephen Covey shares some startling statistics. According to his research, only 22 percent of polled employees agree that workers are focused on organizational goals, and only 23 percent agree that organizational strategy and goals are understood by everyone. These percentages are scary. Are you doing enough to communicate with your employees? Do you take the time to share goals and strategies—daily, weekly, monthly? Do you share information in a variety of formats? Employees like to know what is going on. When Lehman Brothers collapsed and filed for bankruptcy in September of 2008, most of its employees were devastated. When they arrived for work on Monday morning, they had no idea that the business had declared bankruptcy and they no longer had jobs. If employees had been better educated and informed about what was going on, maybe they could have implemented practices or worked with the Securities and Exchange Commission to save the business.

On most corporate Web sites, you can download and listen to investor presentations. Encourage your employees to do this.

There are so many ways to keep employees informed! Here are a few:

- meetings
- conference calls
- webinars
- mailings
- town hall conference calls
- e-mail
- blogs

---

1   *The 8th Habit*, page 370-371.

- video
- performance discussions

12. Conduct effective meetings.

Too many people are spending too much time in unproductive meetings—and those meetings are not fun! If you have to have a meeting, make sure it is a good one. Here are a few questions that will help you plan your meeting.

Why?

Why is the meeting being held? What tasks are planned? What is the overall goal of the meeting and the expected deliverables? What is on the agenda? Is the meeting only a part of a larger goal? Has this goal been written down? Is a project to be selected in the course of the meeting?

Who?

Who is invited? If decisions need to be made, are the right people going to be present? Who is not going to be there? How will attendance affect the successful completion of tasks? Who are the negative people? Who is going to facilitate the meeting? Who is responsible for the agenda? Do the participants know each other? How well? What is the history of the participants? How long have they been meeting?

When?

When is the meeting scheduled? How long should it be? Is there enough time? If the meeting is to be held close to lunch or dinnertime, should it be catered? How much time can be allotted for each agenda item?

Where?

Where is the meeting to be held? Do you and the participants need directions, or lodging or airline recommendations? Are adequate resources available? How is the room arranged? Is the room appropriate for the task? You might decide that it would be better to have the meeting outside on the lawn.

Logistics

What does the meeting cost? Is it money and time well spent? Can people participate via a conference call?

The meeting agenda is the document that defines what will be done at any particular meeting. It should include the following:

- date
- time
- location and directions if needed
- objective of the meeting
- list of tasks to be addressed
- names of participants

Meeting agendas help participants know what to expect and how to prepare for the meeting. The facilitator uses the agenda prior to the meeting to determine specific processes to be used, and during the meeting to keep discussions on track. In order to assure that the meeting will end on time, it is a good practice to allot times for each task or agenda item. If the agenda has not been prepared and distributed, the facilitator should find a way to get the pertinent information to all attendees, to ensure that the necessary people attend and that they come prepared.

Once information about the meeting is assembled, the facilitator can start planning. During the planning stage, the facilitator needs to decide which tool or technique to use where. For example, although a voting system for decision-making is fast and efficient, it may leave too many people dissatisfied with the result. Therefore, more discussion or consensus-building may be called for. A skilled facilitator is crucial to running an effective meeting.

If the meeting gets out of hand, it is the facilitator's job to guide the meeting back on track as quickly as possible. There are a few situations that can occur during a meeting which become distracting and require intervention. These situations are as follows:

- **Side-bar conversations** (when two or more people are having their own discussion). The facilitator can stop speaking. This will create silence in the room, which will allow the rest of the audience to hear the side-bar conversation. The facilitator can also ask the offenders to share what they are discussing with the rest of the group, or he can simply ask them to abide by the established ground rules and keep quiet. If the offenders keep talking, the facilitator can politely ask them to leave.
- **Straying from the topic.** It is the facilitator's job to keep the meeting on track. If a participant pulls the meeting off track by excessive talking, the facilitator can record the issue on a flipchart hanging on the wall (park it in a parking lot), then refer to the agenda and move on.
- **Never-ending discussion.** There comes a time when the facilitator must use judgment to end a discussion. Just do it!
- **Conflict (personal attacks).** The facilitator must immediately interrupt a person when he or she starts to insult or make personal attacks on another. Remind the audience about the ground rules. Do not allow this kind of behavior during a meeting. If the behavior persists, ask the offender to leave. If he doesn't leave, call security.

When returning from breaks, start and end on time. Use a visible timer that everyone can see. You can establish consequences for returning late from a break; for example, state in the ground rules that if anyone is late, he or she has to sing "Take Me Out to the Ballgame" in the front of the room.

13. Provide quality equipment, tools and clothing.

When employees work with well-maintained tools and quality equipment, they are more productive and less frustrated. Years ago, I visited a chemical plant in Canada where the operators were complaining about their company jackets. The company bought new jackets for the operators, but the new jackets weren't as warm as the old ones. (It can get pretty cold working outdoors in Canada!) The old, warm jackets quickly became prized possessions.

Giorgio Armani expects its sales associates to wear Giorgio Armani clothing when they are working, and to adhere to a strict grooming policy. To keep the sales associates happy, the company provides a substantial clothing allowance for its employees.

Every year around Christmas time, New York City Police officers receive a uniform allowance to cover the cost of their uniforms. Years ago, the allowance wasn't taxed; each officer received about $1000 a few weeks before Christmas. Today, taxes are taken out of the uniform allowance, and the officers receive much less. If you are going to provide a benefit, don't be cheap about it!

14. Feed your employees.

Everybody appreciates a good meal. Food is a big deal! I have spoken to thousands of people about creating a motivating work environment, and the subject of food always comes up. People like to eat. They like it more when the food is free or subsidized, and they like it even better when the food is good. Picnics, holiday parties, buffet lunches and ice cream socials are all good ideas.

Every spring, Crystal Run Healthcare in Orange County, New York, hosts barbecue luncheons and dinners at all its sites and gives out gifts.

For the past five years, Dr. Nicholas Pennings of Horizon Family Medical Practice and his wife Carol have hosted a luau at their lake house for their entire staff. They roast a pig, provide entertainment, canoes and rowboats for their guests and encourage the staff to bring family members.

At SAS,[2] a software supplier in Cary, North Carolina, they have a few food traditions: fresh fruit on Monday, M&M's on Wednesday and breakfast goodies on Friday.

Google (listed by *Fortune Magazine* in 2007 as one of the best companies to work for) is known for providing over-the-top perks

---

2   *Fortune Magazine,* February 2009.

for its employees. Years ago, Google's food service program received a lot of positive press. Unlike most other large companies, which contract their food service out to large caterers, Google took charge of its food service, offering free gourmet meals three times a day to its employees and providing tantalizing dishes at 11 on-campus cafes. In 2008, Google cut back their food program a bit; they no longer provide free meals three times a day.

The best employee cafeteria I ever ate at was in Ravenna, Italy, at the Chemtura Chemical Plant. The cafeteria was subsidized by the company, the portions were huge and the food was incredible. The pasta was better than any pasta at any restaurant in the United States. The Italians took the food for granted; it was just what they were used to. I, on the other hand, was amazed.

Over time, the benefit of feeding employees will far outweigh the cost of the food. Well-fed employees will be happier, more productive, and loyal. I don't have any data to support this statement, but it sure sounds good! My daughter used to work as a busgirl at Catherine's, an upscale restaurant in our town. One reason she loved working there was that she ate before her shift.

15. Provide perks for your employees.

Employees love to be taken care of. On-site dry cleaning, subsidized lunches, personal use of company cars, corporate credit cards, gym memberships, adoption assistance, on-site and backup child-care services, parking spaces, gas cards, paid sabbaticals, subsidized elder care, domestic-partner benefits, employee discounts on products and services, stock options and anything else that might benefit your diverse workforce are all good ideas.

At KPMG, employees are eligible to participate in the Mariloff Diamond wholesale discount program. This program makes it possible for employees to purchase fine jewelry and certified loose diamonds at wholesale prices.

At Patagonia, employees can take up to four months off without pay annually to take care of personal business. During that time, Patagonia pays to keep up the employee's health-care coverage and professional dues. For employees pursuing one of the company's environmental internships to preserve beaches or wilderness land, the time comes with full pay.

At Freedom One Financial Group, a Michigan provider of 401(k) plans, employees can earn prizes, free trips and gift certificates for participating in its wellness challenges and losing weight. At the end of a three-month weight challenge, 36 of the company's 70 employees had lost a total of 310 pounds, and 21 employees were given a free cruise.

Aflac is the provider of the largest on-site day care in the state of Georgia. More than 500 children are taken care of at two centers, and the sites are open until 11:30 p.m. to accommodate the second shift.

Alston & Bird, an Atlanta law firm, provides special parking for pregnant moms, on-site child care and a "maternity closet" to recycle clothing.

At Zappos,[3] an online retailer, the CEO is intent on keeping his employees and customers happy. Employee perks include free lunch, regular happy hours, a nap room, profit sharing and fully-paid health benefits. There is also a life coach on site to listen to employees gripe and to help them with their career plans. Customers receive free shipping, thank-you notes and, sometimes, flowers.

In 2008, each employee at King's Daughters Medical Center in Ashland, Kentucky, received an appreciation letter from the CEO. Tucked inside each letter was cash—a $50 bill for part-timers and a $100 bill for full-timers.

According to a recent study by the human resources consulting firm Ceridian, one of the perks most often requested is a casual dress code. Employees consider this a real benefit to the job, allowing them to save money that they would otherwise have to spend on suits. Casual dress also means a higher level of comfort in the office, which can lead to happier employees and increased productivity. While it may not be a practical move in all industries, employers who can offer even one casual day

---

3 *Fortune Magazine*, February 2009, page 58.

per week are likely to see a positive effect on recruitment and retention.

Just understanding that employees have a life outside the office, which sometimes needs attention, is a wonderful perk. If an employee has to take an elderly parent to a doctor's appointment, you don't want the employee to worry about negative consequences at work.

16. Provide massages for your employees.

Since 1997, Stress Recess has provided more than a million massages to employees at places like Coke and Intel. In 2001, Stress Recess became the first chair-massage company to go national, delivering massages over a holiday weekend to beleaguered Delta Airlines agents in Atlanta, New York, Los Angeles, Washington, Dallas and eight more U.S. cities. For more information, go to www. stressrecess.com

17. Hire talented, enthusiastic people and give them feedback.

In his best-selling book *Good to Great*, Jim Collins talks about having the right people on the bus. As a matter of fact, he states that as long as you have the right people on the bus, it isn't necessary to create a motivating work environment, because the right people are self-motivated. Gil Eagles, of Eagles Talent Connection, wrote to me that "A major criterion for bringing on a new team member, besides their qualifications, is their attitude towards being helpful and for getting along with others. There is no room in our small organization for sourpusses or prima donnas."

Never underestimate the power of putting together a team of the right people. Highly competent people with poor attitudes are not going to get you and your organization the results you need. Highly competent people with the right attitudes will exceed performance expectations. Often, teams made up of average people with good attitudes will outperform teams comprised of competent people with poor attitudes. When you make a hiring mistake and hire the wrong person, do everyone a favor—get rid of the wrong person as quickly as possible!

Consider the following combinations:

High competence	+	poor attitude
High competence	+	good attitude
Medium competence	+	good attitude
Medium competence	+	poor attitude
Low competence	+	great attitude

If you had to select two of the above combinations, which would you select? The first answer is easy: most people would select the team members with a high degree of competence and good attitudes. What is the next-best combination? Many people would argue that they would rather have a team with medium competency and great attitudes than a team with high competency and poor attitudes.

Look at what happened during the 1980 Winter Olympics. The United States Hockey team, a group of college and amateur athletes, beat the long-dominant and heavily favored Soviet Union team in a match held on February 22, 1980, at Lake Placid, New York. The United States went on to win the gold medal, beating Finland 4-2 in their final game. The Unites States was clearly the underdog when it came to talent, and they were skating against the Soviet Union, who breathe hockey. What the Americans lacked in talent, they made up for in heart. Was it luck that they won the Olympic Gold, or was it because they had the right attitude?

For centuries, people have been working together in teams. Quite simply, you can get more done in less time when you have a committed team focused on a common goal. Effective teams decide how to move forward as a team. Many follow the plan-do-check-act (PDCA) process while operating as a team. PDCA is an iterative four-step problem-solving process typically used in business process improvement. It is also known as the Deming Cycle, Shewhart cycle, or Deming Wheel.

Other benefits of teamwork include the following:

- improved problem solving
- employee empowerment
- employee development
- improved business processes
- increased creativity which leads to more ideas
- better, cheaper, faster results

Providing feedback to your team will promote productivity. Employees will improve their performance when they know that someone is paying attention and expecting more from them.

Who should receive feedback?

Be sure that the receiver:

- has the ability to develop new skills
- can accept constructive feedback
- has the desire to improve job performance
- believes that your intent is helpful
- respects your opinion

What needs to be heard?

When providing feedback, communicate the employee's skill, strengths, the aspects of his or her performance that exceed or fail to meet expectations, the impact of his or her behavior on others and any developmental opportunities. Be as specific as possible. Share data if it is available.

Share positive feedback as often as you can. Unfortunately, many of us are quick to point out mistakes but not fast enough when it comes to compliments.

Where can feedback be given?

When sharing constructive feedback, try to find a private place where there will be no interruptions. Avoid places where co-workers will hear. Avoid the hallway and noisy lunchroom. Feedback that is entirely positive can be shared in a public or private place.

When is feedback appropriate?

Offer feedback when a project is finished, when a task appears difficult, during a performance discussion, when an employee looks stressed or when a change is being considered. Initiate the discussion when the employee has a willingness to listen.

How should you give feedback?

Providing feedback can be challenging. Usually, feedback is given after an employee has been observed. Once feedback has been received, the employee's behavior sometimes gets worse before it gets better. The employee has to be ready to listen to the feedback and commit to improving his or her performance in order for behavior to change.

Be constructive when you give feedback and express confidence in the employee's ability to improve. For example, don't say, "You really messed that up by skipping this step." Instead, say, "Each step is critical to the success of the project. The next time you do this, make sure all the steps are followed."

18. Create fun.

Provide company picnics, whitewater rafting trips, holiday parties, movie days and other events and outings for your employees. You can plan events on site, such as a scavenger hunt, a treasure hunt or a PaintFest, or you can go off site to a neutral location. During these activities and events, employees will strengthen their relationships and build their network, which will ultimately lead to improved productivity. It's best to offer these events as optional activities. Not everyone wants to raft down a raging river with the boss. As a matter of fact, some employees might get the urge to toss the boss overboard, which is not what you want to happen. The goal of an outing or event should be to encourage teamwork. These events can last one hour or one week; it's up to you. A number of organizations offer structured team-building events for corporations. One such organization is Teambonding. You can reach them at (781)-793-9700 or toll-free at 1.888.398.TEAM (8326). They have a wide variety of programs to encourage team-building.

The Brace Place, with three locations in New Jersey, is a great place to work. The orthodontists at The Brace Place treat their staff to all-expense-paid vacations every few years. The staff, which includes almost sixty people, has gone to Bermuda, Las Vegas, Puerto Rico, Cancun and other resort locations.

A few years ago, The Magic Hat Brewing Company in South Burlington, Vermont decided to organize a Mardi Gras parade on Church Street, a pedestrian walkway in downtown Burlington. Vermont is home to the University of Vermont, Champlain College, Community College of Vermont and St. Michael's College, among other colleges and universities, and you can imagine that after a long, cold winter, local residents and college students are ready for a party. The Mardi Gras parade includes floats, lots of beads and lots of fun. The best part is that the money raised benefits the Women's Rape Crisis Center in Burlington.

19. Host a PaintFest or Build-A-Bike, or support Habitat for Humanity.

John Feight started the Foundation for Hospital Art in 1984. He has traveled around the world with his staff and volunteers for more than 25 years organizing PaintFests. The mission of the Foundation for Hospital Art is to place artwork in every hospital worldwide, to provide comfort for the patients. You can help by hosting a PaintFest at your worksite. You can order a PaintFest kit, which comes with pre-drawn designs, paint supplies and instructions, or you can schedule a customized PaintFest with staff members sent out for event management by the Foundation for Hospital Arts. A PaintFest can be organized for any number of people from 12 to 2,000, or even more. Organizations that have hosted PaintFests include the United States Military Academy, General Electric, American Express, the University of Notre Dame (the student athletes had a PaintFest the day before they played Army), Federal Home Loan Bank and Intel. These are fun events in which everyone can participate for a great cause. For more information, call 770-645-1717 or go to www. hospitalart.org.

Several team-building organizations offer Build-A-Bike kits. Sometimes they partner with non-profits, such as Big Brothers, Big Sisters or the Boys and Girls Club, and give the completed bikes to local kids. During the Build-A-Bike session, each team has puzzles to solve, codes to decipher and secrets to unlock in order to acquire the resources they need, part by part, to build a bicycle. For more information, contact the Leaders Institute at 1-800-872-7830.

Since its founding in 1976 by Millard and Linda Fuller, Habitat for Humanity International has built and rehabilitated more than 250,000 houses working with families in need, becoming a true world leader in addressing the issue of poverty housing. Corporations can form a partnership with Habitat for Humanity in numerous ways, offering product donations or financial support, mobilizing employees as Habitat volunteers, or through a combination of these possibilities. For more information on forming a corporate partnership with Habitat for Humanity International, contact Corporate Programs, Habitat for Humanity International, 121 Habitat St., Americus, Georgia 31709, USA, or phone 1-800-HABITAT (800-422-4828), ext. 7667, or e-mail CorporatePartnerships@hfhi.org.

20. Support good causes.

Give to the community. Become a company that employees are proud to work for. When Hurricane Katrina hit the Gulf Coast in 2005, Chemtura immediately provided resources for the employees at their two chemical plants in the area. When I visited both plants and had a chance to speak with some of the hurricane victims, it became clear to me that Chemtura employees truly cared about their co-workers and rebuilding their community.

Some companies take community service and philanthropy very seriously: they pay their employees to participate in volunteer activities. AT&T encourages its employees to give back to the community by participating in its Community Connections program, which concentrates its efforts in the areas of public safety, community education and lifelong learning, and enhancing family communication.

Every community has yearly races, fairs and events to raise money for cancer, diabetes, autism, etc. Sponsor a team to represent your organization. Give them T-shirts and encouragement. They'll have fun.

21. Encourage wellness.

The cost of health care is a disaster for employees and employers. We must figure out a way to provide affordable health care to our employees, and we must encourage our employees to live a healthy lifestyle. Healthy employees are more valuable, they have more energy, they show up at work when they are supposed to and they cost less to employ. Investing to keep your employees healthy and working beats paying for them when they are out sick. You can provide the following:

- wellness programs
- on-site health screenings
- weight-loss programs
- seminars on health-related topics (diabetes, stress management, healthy cooking)
- walking clubs
- on-site fitness centers
- personal trainers
- free flu shots
- free physical exams
- one-on-one health coaching
- anything else you can think of to encourage healthy living

According to a 2009 article in *Fortune Magazine*,[4] Wegmans Food Markets is rolling out free yoga classes at each of its stores. Maybe yoga is something your employees also would enjoy.

---

4 *Fortune Magazine.* February 2, 2009, page 71.

At the Vermont Teddy Bear factory in Burlington, Vermont, the seamstresses have scheduled stretching breaks where they stand up away from their sewing machines and go through a series of stretches together. Looking down and sewing for eight hours is hard work, and the stretching gives each seamstress an opportunity to relax for a few moments.

22. Offer stress-busters.

Work can be a stressful place, especially today, as we move through the worst recession our country has seen since the Great Depression. Some occupations are stressful by nature: emergency-room workers, police officers, prison guards and miners are a few groups who experience more stress than most other employees. During today's economic crisis, other occupations, too, can be perceived as being highly stressful: stockbrokers, realtors, automotive workers, car salespeople and retail sales managers are all experiencing higher levels of workplace stress. Small-business owners are also in a precarious position when the economy slows down.

Some stress is good. It motivates us and makes us stronger. Too much stress is bad. It makes us irrational and grouchy, and it can quite literally kill us. Fortunately, you can do specific things to help reduce and better cope with stress at work.

- Take care of yourself. Make sure that you eat right, exercise and get enough sleep. Take advantage of your company's wellness programs.
- Count your blessings. You may be out of work or nervous about losing your job, but you are capable of doing good work. You have your health, your education and your experience, which no one can take away from you. Make a list of everything that is good in your life.
- Ask for help when you need it. Most employers provide assistance through Employee Assistance Programs (EAPs). If you do not have access to an EAP, ask your spouse, your

brother or your minister for help. No one wants to see you suffer in silence.

- Schedule a visit to your doctor if stress is leading to panic attacks, anxiety or depression.

Do something fun. Plan a date with a friend, go for a hike, play golf, attend a concert, quilt, get a manicure. Go boating, bird watching or shopping, cook a great meal, play with your kids, sign up for a class, call an old friend, make a scrapbook or try something new—just for the fun of it.

23. Offer an espresso bar and/or gourmet coffee.

Coffee is a big deal to coffee drinkers. I'm too cheap to spend five dollars on an extra-tall Frappuchino at Starbucks, but my kids don't think twice about it. They are Generation X employees. They know more about coffee, cappuccino and espresso than I ever will. They grind their own coffee beans and spend hours talking about the best way to brew a cup of coffee. I was at a chemical plant in Italy that had an espresso bar right next to the cafeteria, and it was common practice for the men to smoke and sip espresso after lunch.

24. Provide sign-on bonuses and perks.

When Christus Santa Rosa Healthcare hires nurse managers, they give them a "Welcome to San Antonio" package, which includes these perks:

- four passes to Six Flags
- four passes to a San Antonio Spurs game
- dinner for four on the Riverwalk
- four passes to the San Antonio Zoo
- four passes to Sea World
- four passes to a San Antonio Missions baseball game

25. Maintain a solid reputation.

Every year, extensive employee surveys are conducted to determine the best companies to work for. *Fortune Magazine* publishes their Top 100 Employers list every February. In 2008, NetApp, a data storage and management company based in Sunnyvale, California, took the coveted number one spot after six years on the list. Vanderbilt University in Nashville, Tennessee, also appeared on the 2008 list. It was the first time an educational institution had appeared on the list. At Vanderbilt University, employees and their dependents receive a seventy percent tuition subsidy to any college in the country.

Working Mother Magazine has a few lists of its own: the Best Green Company, the Best Company for Multicultural Women, the Best Law Firms for Women, the Best Women-Owned Companies and the 100 Best Companies. In 2008, the top ten companies on the 100 Best Companies list were Abbott, Baptist Health South Florida, Bristol-Myers Squibb, Ernst & Young, IBM, KPMG, The McGraw-Hill Company, Pillsbury Winthrop Shaw Pittman, PricewaterhouseCoopers and S.C. Johnson & Son.

You have to apply to get on these lists. Some companies have public relations people who spend a great deal of their time compiling survey data for these lists. To be eligible for the *Fortune Magazine* list, you must have at least 1000 U.S. employees and be at least seven years old. To nominate your company, go to www.greatplacetowork.com.

Many states also publish lists. In 2004, Best Companies Group (BCG) was formed with the purpose of identifying and recognizing the best employers within a region and industry. BCG partners with media and/or publication entities, human resources groups, chambers of commerce and economic organizations to publicize their endeavor, encourage participation and recognize those who make the Best Places to Work list. BCG is a division of Journal Publications Inc (JPI), a multi-title publishing and events company located in Harrisburg, Pennsylvania.

There is no down side to being included on any of these lists. When you are included, your employees will be proud that they work for such a reputable organization, and recruiting new employees will be easier.

26. Offer employees an Employee Assistance Program (EAP).

Employee Assistance Programs are employee benefit programs offered by many employers, typically in conjunction with a health insurance plan. EAPs are intended to help employees deal with personal problems that might adversely impact their work performance, health and well-being. EAPs generally include assessment, short-term counseling and referral services to additional resources for employees and their household members.

These programs are becoming increasingly common in today's work sites. As the field grows, the responsibilities of employee assistance professionals are expanding as well. Many EAP experts have expressed deep concern over the numerous ethical and quality issues existing in the field today. The issues for which EAPs provide support vary, but examples include the following:

- substance abuse
- safe work environment
- emotional distress
- coping with major life events, including births, accidents and deaths
- health care concerns
- financial or legal concerns
- family or personal-relationship issues
- work relationship issues
- concerns about aging parents

27. Value diversity.

Diverse cultures, diverse people and diverse thinking are what make the world go round. The world seems to be getting smaller and smaller these days, and the success of any organization depends upon the ability of its people to work together to achieve a common goal. People will effectively work together when they feel valued and respected for who they are and what they bring to the table. Twice a year, in Columbus, Indiana, Cummins Engine Company brings its Master Black Belts from around the globe together to meet with and learn from each other. These weeklong events, called Master Black Belt symposiums, provide an opportunity for all the Master Black Belts to learn about diverse cultures and global business.

Many organizations have Diversity Managers, whose sole responsibility is to make sure the organization is focused and fair when dealing with a diverse workforce.

28. Allow employees to worship and pray as they choose.

If an employee wants to take a personal day on Good Friday or Yom Kippur, let him. If an employee wants to wash his feet in the bathroom sink or set out a prayer rug, it would be a good idea to give him some personal space.

29. Have fair and consistent policies and procedures.

Everyone wants to feel that he or she is being treated fairly by an organization. Hire ethical leaders who understand the difference between right and wrong. These ethical leaders must be able to administer policies and procedures consistently. If they don't, chaos and frustration will follow.

30. Provide competitive benefits packages and fair wages.

Enough said!

31. Provide the latest and greatest technology that you can afford.

At Sigma Breakthrough Technologies Inc., a camera system was installed to link the New Jersey and Texas offices. During weekly meetings, all the people in both offices can see each other. Joe

Ficalora, President of SBTI Global Services, says, "It's a good motivator because we can see what they are seeing, and vice-versa."

In 2008, the staff at Google received brand new Dream Phones, the iPhone challenger that runs Google's Android software.

32. Have a continuous-improvement culture.

A continuous-improvement culture is about making work better every day for your employees. Although the concepts of continuous improvement and measurement have been around for quite a while, there are still many, many people in many, many organizations who just don't get it. These people have never been exposed to continuous-improvement thinking and/or have never been held accountable for making a process better. My experience has been that you need to share process-improvement success stories with others, and the stories need to be relevant to the particular industry. If you are working in a hospital, sharing stories about manufacturing isn't going to work. You need to find hospital/health care success stories. Compare apples to apples! If you are working with a government agency, you need to benchmark what is happening in other government agencies. The City of Fort Wayne, Indiana has done a tremendous job in using process-improvement methodology to save taxpayers millions of dollars. During the fall of 2006, I delivered a one-day program for the Government of Orange County, New York titled "An Introduction to Process Improvement," and I introduced examples from the City of Fort Wayne, Indiana to convince the Orange County Commissioners that process improvement was a worthwhile goal.

Continuous-improvement concepts have been around since the early days of manufacturing in Japan. Toyota's world-class manufacturing systems grew out of a culture of continuous improvement. The Japanese refer to this thinking as *kaizen*, which means "doing things better every day." This world view was derived from an economy of scarcity: Toyota could not afford excess waste. In 1950, Toyota's near-bankruptcy in a difficult year further refined its philosophy of frugality. Toyota soon became obsessively focused on reducing *muda*, or waste, and building up a vast storehouse of cash for security. Edward Deming, an expert in quality control, once said, "If you can't describe what you are doing as a process, then you don't know what you are doing."

33. Hire ethical leaders.

Employees want to work for leaders they trust. They want to work for leaders who are honest and smart, who have integrity and will do the right thing in good times and, especially, turbulent times.

It seems as if every week we read another story about a greedy, unethical leader. It's hard for me to believe that Timothy Geithner was sworn in as the United States Treasury Secretary on January 26, 2009, after admitting that he failed to pay his taxes. Mr. Geithner's credibility is tarnished because he chose not to pay his taxes—something every American citizen is supposed to do by April 15th of every calendar year! One could argue that the reason our economy is in such a mess right now is because financial leaders got too greedy and lost their moral compass. Instead of making sure that people could afford mortgages, they were handing out loans to unqualified buyers and padding their own pockets. Bernard Madoff is one of the most recent examples of a white-collar crook. He robbed people by masterminding the largest Ponzi scam of all time. Bernard Ebbers, the former chairman and founder of WorldCom, was sentenced to 25 years in prison for his role in an $11 billion fraud that bankrupted his telecommunications company. Kenneth Lay, the founder of Enron, was put on trial for fraud and conspiracy. Dennis Kozlowski, the former chief executive of Tyco, was convicted of misappropriating more than $400 million of the company's funds. He is currently serving at least eight years and four months in prison. It was reported in early 2009 that Merrill Lynch CEO John Thain spent hundreds of thousands of dollars decorating his office while Merrill Lynch prepared to slash expenses, cut thousands of jobs and exit businesses to fix the ailing securities firm.

34. Set stretch goals for your employees.

You will never know what your employees are capable of unless you give them stretch goals. In the movie *Twelve O'Clock High*, Gregory Peck played the part of a hard-as-nails general who had to push his pilots to see what they were capable of. The character he played wasn't well liked by the troops, but he was able to accomplish a great deal by setting stretch goals for his pilots. In his book *Good to Great*, Jim Collins talks about good performance being the enemy of great performance. If "good" is good enough, why would anyone push himself to "great"? When you set stretch goals, you encourage your employees to move out of their comfort zone and reach for what they think is impossible.

35. Create a team atmosphere.

Reward team performance in addition to individual performance. For centuries, people have been working together in teams. You can simply get more done in less time when you have a committed team focused on a common goal.

A team is much more than a group of people coming together. A team has a common purpose or mission, is committed to the mission and places the team goal above individual glory. Whether on the playing field or in the workplace, teams develop and mature over time. If you have ever watched little children play soccer, you will understand the concept of people coming together and defining their roles and responsibilities. In the beginning of the season, all the kids gather around the ball, and each one tries to make contact with it. They fall over each other, creating chaos on the field. They understand the team's goal but are not sure how to reach it. The roles of the team members are not yet clear. As the team practices and matures, the members realize that they can't all go after the ball at the same time. It just doesn't work!

There are many different models of team development. One of the most widely used models, developed by Bruce Tuckman in 1965 when he was working for the United States Naval Medical Research Institute, is called the "orming" model. In this model, the team leader begins with a very hands-on approach but adopts a more supportive role as the team develops and matures.

		Desired outcome
Forming	Members are selected. Goals are unclear. Not building on each other's ideas yet. People are polite to avoid conflict.	Commitment to goal. Desire to be part of the team.
Storming	Chaos occurs. Conflict arises. Defensiveness and finger pointing can occur. Goals may be unclear. Team may claim that the problem can't be solved.	Clarification of problems & positions. Belonging with team mates.
Norming	Team members are committed to the task. They feel comfortable with each other and enjoy working together.	Involvement with solving problems. Supporting others.
Performing	Team members are completely interdependent. Teams develop innovative problem solving. Members understand each others feelings.	Achievement through team effort. Pride in team mates.

36. Manage conflict in a timely manner.

No one likes conflict. We don't like conflict in our personal lives and we don't like conflict in our professional lives. Many family relationships become strained because no one was willing or able to deal with conflict. There are brothers and sisters, mothers and daughters, fathers and sons who haven't spoken to each other in years because of conflict. I know that you are reading this and thinking about people you know who live with strained relationships. At work, we must deal with conflict; we don't have the luxury of ignoring it and hoping it will eventually go away. Good bosses deal with conflict in a timely fashion. As soon as they see or hear about a problem, they directly approach the people involved and work out a plan for conflict resolution. Every manager and supervisor should receive basic training in conflict resolution.

37. Provide a mentoring program.

In most organizations, informal mentoring goes on all the time. Years ago, when I was a corporate employee, the Chief Financial Officer spent time teaching me how to read financial documents and the annual report. I was so appreciative of the time he took to mentor me. Mentoring can be of real value to employees. If you don't already have a formal mentoring program, consider starting one. A good mentoring program can help you reduce employee turnover and develop your high-potential candidates more quickly. You can find good materials for designing programs and training mentors and mentees on the Web. Consider bringing in one or more consultants to help you think through your strategy, train people and evaluate the impact of the mentoring effort. There are even online mentoring programs available, which might work well with Generation X and Y employees.

38. Get rid of problem employees.

At one time or another, every recruiter makes a bad hiring decision. Problem employees cause headaches, aggravation and frustration for those who work with them, for them and around them. Great organizations fire people who cause problems. They fire them legally and quickly. I do quite a bit of work in health care, and I've observed that health care is one of those industries that puts up with problem employees. It seems that as long as a person has good clinical skills, the health care organization is willing to put up with bad behavior. A few years, the CEO of a hospital hired me to coach a Chief Nursing Officer who yelled at nurses and made them cry. She was nasty, she knew it and she got away with it, and the CEO wasn't willing to fire her. When you allow problem employees to keep their jobs, you send the wrong message to other employees. You communicate that bad behavior is acceptable.

39. Use self-deprecating humor.

Many comedians and professional speakers use self-deprecating humor to avoid seeming arrogant or pompous and to help the audience identify with them. You can use self-deprecating humor in the workplace to build relationships with others. For example, you can say to a co-worker, "I'm really terrible at keeping things organized. I'd like you to work on this project with me because I know you are better at organizing than I am and I can use all the help that I can get."

40. Don't micromanage.

Micromanagement has a negative effect on employees. Bosses who micromanage create stress for their workers and increase employee turnover. There is no reason to constantly look over someone's shoulder. Trust your employees to do a good job. When they make mistakes—and they will—focus on the lessons learned from the mistakes. When you allow people to learn from their mistakes, you are developing them as future leaders.

41. Give credit where it's due.

In 1993, when Walter Payton was inducted into the National Football League Hall of Fame, he thanked his teammates for providing the holes in the field so that he could run. Walter Payton was a talented running back, who missed one game as a rookie player and then played in 186 consecutive games. He worked hard and deserved to be inducted into the Hall of Fame. Walter decided to give his teammates the credit.

42. Send a handwritten thank-you note.

When was the last time you received a handwritten note from a co-worker, boss, vendor or supplier? How did it make you feel? I have asked this question to many employees during management training seminars. The answer is always the same: people rarely send handwritten notes, and when they do they are greatly appreciated. A handwritten note implies that the writer thought highly enough of the reader to take the time to write a note.

43. Reimburse employees quickly for their out-of-pocket expenses.

Have a fair employee-reimbursement policy. Many employees incur out-of-pocket expenses for a variety of reasons: corporate travel, cell phone bills, client meals, home business phone lines, home internet connection expenses, etc. Have a policy that not only covers the expenses but pays employees in a timely manner. The policy should cover all the employees who incur expenses, not just senior executives.

44. Provide company sponsored transportation.

Wouldn't it be great if you could hop on a bus, van or train that took you from your home directly to your place of employment for free or for a reduced fare?

Many organizations provide free car service and/or drivers for their senior executives, while the rest of the workforce has to figure out the most cost-effective way to travel to and from work. In major cities such as New York, Chicago and Atlanta, employees travel on crowded trains, subways, buses and ferryboats. Public transportation in major cities is expensive and not always reliable. When an employer provides free transportation home, it is a big deal—especially for working girls, who aren't always comfortable traveling alone.

45. Provide a company matching program when your employees make charitable donations.

46. Support community events by providing sponsorship dollars.

ING is the major sponsor of the New York City Marathon. On Marathon Sunday, which is always in November, the employees of ING gather in Central Park and other parts of the Marathon route to cheer the runners, provide support for the New York Road Runners Club and have a fun day.

Macy's sponsors many great events: the Thanksgiving Day Parade, the Fourth of July fireworks display over the East River in New York, and the annual Flower Show are just a few. For over eighty years, Macy's Thanksgiving Day Parade—"the longest show on Broadway"—has been the official kick-off of the holiday season. Every year, the parade is seen by more than three million people who line the streets of New York and another fifty million who tune into NBC and Telemundo to watch the giant balloons, the one-of-a-kind floats, the nation's best marching bands, the hundreds of cheering clowns and a host of celebrities. During the Thanksgiving Day Parade, employees from every Macy's store are invited to participate in the parade as clowns, balloon handlers and support people. In 1986, I was a training manager for Macy's New York, and I had the opportunity to walk in the parade as a balloon handler for Superman. My husband walked with me, and we had an incredible day. I still go to the parade every year with my kids. It has become a Thanksgiving Day tradition for our family.

47. Offer flexible work arrangements.

Employees like to have options and flexibility. If you provide your employees with job sharing, flextime, extended work days and work-from-home options, you will be a sought-after employer. One of the greatest barriers to flextime is the reluctance of supervisors who anticipate inadequate staffing and difficulties with communication, meetings, scheduling, supervision and timekeeping. Because certain types of work are not suited to flextime, inequities may result if it is offered to only certain departments or classes of workers. Union opposition arises from the loss of overtime rights; labor legislation regarding overtime hours may constrain certain scheduling arrangements.

You can offer your employees a number of different summer schedules. Some companies keep the regular Monday-to-Thursday work hours and then give employees a half-day off on Friday. This is a nice perk, especially for those employees who like to get a jumpstart on the weekend or avoid Friday beach traffic. Other employers give their employees the option of working extended hours Monday through Thursday so that they can leave work early on Friday.

48. Offer your employees stock options when they exceed performance goals, or as a sign-on bonus.

Years ago, stock options were reserved for senior executives. Today, many rank-and-file employees have gotten wealthy by owning stock options. Offering stock options is a great way to show your employees how much you appreciate their work. Owning stock also makes employees feel like owners or partners in the business.

49. Get rid of fluorescent lighting.

For at least eight hours every day, five days every week, most of us work under lights we would never consider putting in our homes. Headaches, eyestrain, and foggy thinking—symptoms commonly attributed to stress or fatigue—are actually the result of the antiquated fluorescent lighting still used in far too many offices nearly 75 years after its invention, despite overwhelming scientific evidence that it is harmful to people's health.

50. Offer Lunch-'N-Learn programs.

Lunchtime is a great time for employees to relax and recharge their batteries for the remainder of the workday. A Lunch-'N-Learn program is usually 45 to 50 minutes long. Employees can bring a bag lunch, or lunch can be provided by the company. The program can be a one-time event or it can last for a few weeks. Almost any topic is appropriate for a Lunch-'N-Learn; you can offer business-related topics, health-related topics or just fun stuff. You can use internal experts or outside vendors to lead the programs. If you are lucky enough to get senior executives to lead a program, it will be a great success. Here are a few suggestions:

- knitting, crocheting, embroidering or any other how-to that you can think of
- maintaining work/life balance
- flower arranging
- introduction to drawing
- fundamentals of Excel, PowerPoint, Microsoft Word, Outlook or Adobe PhotoShop
- digital photography
- doing business in China, South America, Vietnam, India or any other place
- learning Spanish as a second language
- the do's and don'ts of international travel
- ballroom dancing, tap dancing or line dancing
- Weight Watchers
- wok cooking
- creating a Web site

51. Celebrate holidays.

There are so many holidays and so many fun ways to celebrate them. Lots of organizations allow their employees to dress up for Halloween. I met a lawyer from New Jersey who told me that in her law office they start to plan their Halloween celebration a year in advance. Employees are assigned to a team, and each team has to perform a skit. She also told me that they get no work done that day—but they have lots of fun!

Thanksgiving is a great holiday to celebrate at work. Many organizations host a Thanksgiving lunch, at which the senior executives serve the employees. Or how about having a Veterans' Day lunch to honor all the members of the Armed Forces, or taking employees to a Chinese restaurant in January to celebrate the Chinese New Year?

The 34th Police Precinct in New York City schedules a holiday party for the adults and another holiday party for the cops' kids. The kids' party is at the Columbia University Chrystie Field House in northern Manhattan. There are NYPD horses, helicopters and Emergency Services vehicles for the kids to see. There is also an abundance of food, games and crafts, as well as Santa Claus.

Many people have told me that during the Christmas holiday they have a Secret Santa, grab-bag or white elephant gift exchange within their departments. A fun twist is when the first person chooses a gift, and then the next person can choose to take that gift away or open a new gift. It seems as if there is always one coveted gift everyone wants, which leads to lots of laughs.

At Orange Regional Medical Center in New York, the Radiation Oncology Department goes all out for most holidays, and they try hard to include the patients in the celebrations. They celebrate Valentine's Day, St. Patrick's Day, Inauguration Day in 2009, Mardi Gras, Christmas and other holidays as they occur. Every year, for Easter, Dr. Thomas R. Eanelli, Medical Director and Chairman of the Radiation Oncology Department, purchases chocolate bunnies from the Lion's Club and gives them to the patients. On Valentine's Day, he buys flowers to be given to each of the patients. For Mardi Gras, the staff hands out beads and coins to all the patients. During the month of October, the staff wears pink and makes little tokens for the patients to celebrate Breast Cancer Awareness Month.

Regina M. Clark

52. Establish a formal reward-and-recognition program.

Establishing a formal reward-and-recognition program is part of creating a motivating work environment for your employees. Think of your reward program as a piece of the puzzle. It's not the entire puzzle, although an entire industry has been built around employee reward and recognition. There is even an association for recognition professionals, called Recognition Professionals International, which provides its members with educational conferences and other resources. To find out more about RPI, go to www.recognition.org.

A reward-and-recognition program can help you reward performance, celebrate achievement and honor years of service. A sound recognition strategy can motivate your employees and lead to behavioral change. Studies conducted by the International Society of Performance Improvement have shown that with a correctly implemented and tracked incentive program, productivity can increase by more than twenty percent.

There are many ways to formally reward and recognize employees, and many companies that can work with you to put together an effective reward-and-recognition program. Every year, *HRO Today Magazine* puts out a list of the top employee recognition service providers. In 2008, the list included the following:

Rideau Recognition Solutions, www.rideau.com (1.6 million employees serviced in 2007)
Michael C. Fina, www.mcfawards.com (more than one million employees serviced in 2007)
Diamond H Recognition, www.diamondh.com (more than one million employees serviced in 2007)
Anderson Performance Improvement Company, www.andersonperformance.com (350,000 employees serviced in 2007)
Globoforce, www.globoforce.com (1.7 million employees serviced in 2007)

Perks.com, www.perks.com (more than 3.5 million employees
serviced in 2007)

Rymax Marketing Services, Inc., www.rymaxinc.com (more
than 100,000 employees serviced in 2007)

TharpeRobbins, www.tharpe.com (more than one million
employees serviced in 2007)

O.C. Tanner, www.octanner.com (2.5 million employees
serviced in 2007)

Bennett Brothers, Inc., www.bennettbrothers.com (more
than 250,000 employees serviced in 2007)

IncentOne, www.incentone.com (more than five million
employees serviced in 2007)

Maritz, www.maritz.com (more than 1.5 million employees
serviced in 2007)

The Terryberry Company, www.terryberry.com (550,000
employees serviced in 2007)

In 2008, I spoke at the Society for Human Resources National
Conference in Chicago, Illinois. The exhibit hall was packed with
vendors and suppliers that provide organizations with clocks, tro-
phies, jewelry, key chains, shirts, hats and other stuff that can be
used to reward and recognize employee behavior. You can spend
from $20 to $3000 on one item. One vendor handed me a stuffed
puppy with spots on it. At first, I didn't make the connection. Then
the vendor told me that the puppy, named Spot, was part of their
"On the Spot" recognition program. When selecting a vendor, make
sure that it provides exceptional service and has experience with
being culturally appropriate—a spotted stuffed animal might work
well in New York but not in China! And keep in mind that there is
no such thing as "one size fits all." One employee might be thrilled
to attend a Service Award dinner and receive a plaque; another
employee couldn't care less about the dinner and plaque, but would
love a day off.

53. Send an e-card.

MTM Recognition is an employee recognition company that has been around for years. They help organizations put together recognition strategies that lead to behavioral change and drive success. They specialize in creating custom jewelry. For years, they have designed Super Bowl rings. You can send an e-card from their Web site for free. Go to www.mtmrecognition.com.

54. Celebrate Employee Appreciation Day.

Employee Appreciation Day first arrived on calendars in 1995. Bob Nelson, one of the founding board members of Recognition Professionals International, created Employee Appreciation Day with his publishing company, Workman Publishing, as a way of focusing the attention of employers in all industries on employee recognition. It is always held on the first Friday in March.

55. Host a Service Award event.

Some employees really do like to be recognized for years of service. They appreciate the watch, certificate or crystal paperweight. They like seeing their names in the company newsletter. Other employees couldn't care less. Have a Service Award dinner or luncheon and make it optional. Don't force people to attend, especially if the event is scheduled after normal working hours.

56. Hire a motivational speaker to fire up your employees.

There are thousands of motivational speakers. Some are expensive celebrity speakers, and some will speak for free. Their job is to perform. Good motivational speakers deliver a powerful message that makes your audience do something better. Most credible speakers have a specific expertise; you can find people who speak on leadership, innovation, future trends, technology and every other topic you can think of. How do you find a good motivational speaker? You can start by searching the National Speakers Association Web site, www.nsa-speaker.org. You can conduct a search by topic area, geographical area and price range. If you decide to select a speaker with a Certified Speaking Professional (CSP) designation, you will be sure that he or she is experienced. Fewer than ten percent of professional speakers have the CSP designation. You can also find a speaker by contacting a Speaker Bureau. The International Association of Speaker Bureaus (www.IASBweb.org) will provide you with a list of bureaus. Eagles Talent Connection is a reputable full-service bureau that specializes in helping corporate meeting planners select and present motivational speakers, sports stars, celebrities and corporate entertainment. Their phone number is 973-313-9800.

57. Wear a silly hat, mouse ears or a Hawaiian shirt.

Seven days without laughter make one weak.
—Dr. Joel Goodman, The HUMOR Project

We were all kids once. Why not tap into your inner child and do something silly and fun? Those of you who have young children get to be silly all the time. You get to read Dr. Seuss books, play Go Fish and eat cotton candy. I have three children, aged twenty-four, eighteen and five. My five-year-old keeps me young. A few weeks ago, I went roller-skating for the first time in many, many years. There was one other adult skating, and she clearly knew what she was doing. Most of the adults were standing outside the rink and watching or waving as their children flew by. Not me! I was trying hard to stay vertical on the skates. It was not a pretty sight.

Think about what would happen if you showed up at work with a silly hat on your head—maybe one of the Goofy hats they sell in Disney World, or a red-and-white Cat in the Hat hat, or Mickey Mouse ears. Would people notice? Would they say anything? Would you get a laugh? Would someone else want to try your hat on? Creating levity at work is a good thing, even if it just lasts a moment.

In the movie *Patch Adams*, we watch Robin Williams portray a doctor who believes in laughter as medicine and will do just about anything to make his patients laugh, even if it means risking his own career. He shows up at work dressed as a clown. He plays with the kids and gets them laughing. Convinced of the powerful connection between environment and wellness, Patch believes that the health of an individual cannot be separated from the health of one's family, community and world. The movie *Patch Adams* was based on the true life story of Hunter "Patch" Adams and the book *Gesundheit: Good Health is a Laughing Matter* by Adams and Maureen Mylander.

58. Run with Mickey Mouse.

Get a team together to run in the Walt Disney World Marathon. In January of every year, Walt Disney World hosts the marathon, which winds through the theme parks. It's an entire weekend filled with competition and fun, starting with Disney's Health & Fitness Expo and ending when you cross the finish line to earn the exclusive Mickey Mouse, Donald Duck or Goofy medals. If that doesn't motivate you to new levels of character, nothing will.

59. Escape to a show.

I used to work for a company in Mahwah, New Jersey. Every few months, the company would offer dinner and Broadway show tickets to employees. The bus, which was paid for by the company, would pick us up at 5:00 and drop us off in the theatre district, and it would be waiting for us after the show. For more information about show tickets, go to www.broadwayoffers.com.

60. Participate in the Take Our Daughters And Sons To Work® program.

The national date for the Take Our Daughters And Sons To Work program is always on the fourth Thursday in April; the 2009 program will be on Thursday, April 23rd. The recommended age range for children in the program is eight to eighteen years old. After all, it's pretty distracting to have a toddler running around at the office. The official Web site for this program is www.daughtersandsonstowork.org.

Designed to be more than a career day, the Take Our Daughters And Sons To Work program goes beyond the average "shadow an adult" kids' day at the office. Exposing girls and boys to what a parent or mentor in their lives does during the workday is important; but showing them the value of education, helping them discover the power and possibilities associated with a balanced work and family life, providing them with an opportunity to express how they envision the future and to take the first steps toward their goals in an interactive, hands-on environment is essential to their success.

61. Host a Bring Your Pet to Work Day.

The animal lovers will enjoy this. At Red Barn in Middletown, New York, there are always two big dogs behind the counter, and pictures of customers with their pets cover the wall, including a picture of my three-year-old daughter hugging our chocolate Labrador. Every time I enter the store, I stop to look at the picture (my daughter is now in college, and Coco is in doggy heaven). Just make sure that you establish some rules before allowing pets in the workplace. At Burton Snowboards in Burlington, Vermont, employees must clean up after their canines and remove all pooch evidence from the company's front lawn when the snow melts in the spring.

62. Give your employees a Candy Survival Kit.

The Candy Survival Kit contains a delightful assortment of nostalgic candies, each with a special connection to being a valued employee. These can be ordered at www.dailyapples.com. The candies include a Tootsie Roll Pop to remind employees of the important "role" they play; a Pixy Stix to help employees "pick out" their special qualities and skills; a Candy Watch to thank employees for their "quality time"; pumpkin seeds to help employees "grow" personally and professionally; Smarties to help employees solve challenging problems; a Laffy Taffy to remind employees to laugh; a Candy Lipstick to encourage employees to communicate effectively; a peppermint to recognize employees' "commit-mint" to their jobs; bubblegum to help employees "stick together" to complete any task; and a Satellite Wafer to acknowledge talents that are truly "out of this world."

63. Add music to the work environment.

Music can influence an employee's mood. The right music can have a pleasant or positive effect, and the wrong music can be irritating. How do you select the music? Ask your employees what they like to listen to. Put together an eclectic play list. You can pipe in music through speakers or host a live music event at work. How about a Friday jam session in the cafeteria, or a quarterly concert? You probably have talented musicians on your payroll and don't even know it. If you want to spend some money, you can bring musicians in to entertain your employees during work hours or after work. The session can even be recorded for those who miss it.

64. Schedule some healthy competition.

Some people are competitive by nature. My husband's competitive streak comes out when we play cards, watch Jeopardy, play Trouble with our five-year-old son and on many other occasions. He's just competitive by nature, and he can't help it. Competitive people get fired up when there is a contest, a winner, an opportunity, a challenge or a chance to show their stuff. You can turn just about anything into a competition: weight loss, a new product promotion, a neat office, a ping pong tournament, a quiz bowl, a company-sponsored softball game or streamlining a process to reduce waste. Here are a few ideas for setting up a competition or tournament:

- For years, I have been playing Jeopardy in training classes. Everyone loves to play, and it is a great way to review information. You can set up weekly or monthly tournaments. Game Show Pro is an easy-to-use, inexpensive software program you can purchase that will help you create the Jeopardy Game Board.

- Set up a Wii game station, a pinball machine, a Mini Putt course or a pool table in the employee cafeteria for a week, a month or permanently.
- Play human chess. You can rent a human chessboard and other fun stuff from www.funatwork.com.
- Schedule a golf outing. Golf is a favorite pastime of many; there are over twenty-six million golfers in the United States alone. A golf outing typically includes food, beverages, prizes and sponsors. Everyone can get involved. Employees who don't play golf can drive the golf carts, help with the food, secure sponsors or just relax and cheer others on. The golf course is also a great place to network and build your business relationships. Mike Smith, author of *Business-To-Business Golf,* suggests that mixing business and golf helps solidify relationships.

Just be careful. Those of us who are not competitive can easily get annoyed by the competitive nuts.

65. Measure results.

There is an old saying, "What matters gets measured." If something at work is important to the organization, it should be measured. For example, the airline industry measures on-time departures and landings; the hospitality industry measures customer satisfaction by conducting surveys; the health care industry measures patient satisfaction; the retail industry measures floor space and daily sales. In order to measure something, you must collect data. Once the data is analyzed, the results need to be communicated to the organization. Every process at work can be measured. Competitive people love to measure and post results; it is a way for them to track performance. Collecting and analyzing data to improve your product or service is a good business practice. The Web site www.isixsigma.com has a great deal of material about data collection and measuring.

66. Offer dress down days.

Many organizations jumped on the "casual dress day" bandwagon in the late 1990s. This trend has had mixed reactions. Some articles state that when employees are more comfortable (casual), productivity goes up, while others report the opposite. I suggest that you survey your employees and find out what they prefer. Do they like causal days (also known as dress down days), or are they comfortable with the current dress code? Casual dress does not suite every culture. For one Friday each month, the management of The First National Bank of Jeffersonville, in New York State, encourages employees to wear jeans to work provided that they give a donation to a selected charity. The decision on where the funds go rotates to a different department or branch each month. In 2008, $8,062 was raised for 15 organizations, families or individuals. Some schools that have strict dress codes have also used dress down days to raise funds for charity. When my kids went to Catholic school, they were allowed to wear jeans on dress down days if they brought in one dollar. The girls liked this option; the boys didn't seem to care too much about what they wore.

67. Have a baby photo contest.

A manager at the University of Michigan told me about a baby photo contest within his department. All forty-one employees participated. Each employee brought in a baby photo, which was then scanned into a computer, and all the photos were posted. The winner received a twenty-five-dollar gift certificate to a local restaurant. (A few of the supervisors chipped in for the prize, since the department had no budget for prize money).

68. Add puns to e-mail messages.

Jim Sutton, who works for Mirant, likes to add short puns to his e-mail messages. Jim gets most of his examples from www.bored. com/sillypuns/index.htm. Here are a few examples:

- Did you hear about the optometrist who fell into a lens grinder and made a spectacle of himself?
- There were two ships. One had red paint, one had blue paint. They collided. At last report, the survivors were marooned.
- Why is Saudi Arabia free of mental illness? There are nomad people there.

Before you start adding puns to your e-mail messages, it might be a good idea to check with your employer and make sure that it is okay.

69. Surround yourself with beautiful artwork.

Every community has local artists. Why not support your local artists by purchasing some of their artwork and displaying it in prominent locations in the workplace? According to Linda Hubbard of the River Winds Gallery (www.riverwindsgallery.com), artwork uplifts the whole office. Hanging artwork might also inspire your employees to be more creative and productive.

If you are looking for motivational artwork, check out the Successories Web site at www.successories.com. Successories has a wide variety of motivational posters, prints, coffee mugs, mouse pads, paperweights and other items.

70. Find opportunities for your employees to shine.

Ten years ago, Cummins Inc. decided to implement a corporate-wide Six Sigma initiative. From the start, Cummins Inc. came up with creative ways to reward and recognize participants and teams that were working on Six Sigma projects. They provided shirts, mugs, flashlights, crystal paperweights, laser pointers, bonuses and a wide variety of other trinkets to give to the Black Belts and Green Belts. For those of you not familiar with Six Sigma terminology, a Black Belt is a person who goes through rigorous process-improvement training, typically for four weeks, leads a team and completes a project. A Green Belt usually goes through two weeks of training and completes a project with the help of a Black Belt. A Master Black Belt is an expert who provides coaching and, often, training to Black Belts and Green Belts. Every Six Sigma project is carefully selected, sponsored by a senior executive and tied to improving business results. At the completion of Black Belt training, Cummins Inc. celebrates by having a dinner or lunch with the graduating class. In 2001, Cummins Inc. started to give out Chairman Quality Awards to Black Belts who completed outstanding Six Sigma projects that saved the company money, improved work processes and strengthened teams. In 2001, 14 awards were distributed. Last year, 40 awards were distributed. Yearly, Cummins closes approximately 3000 projects worldwide, so to be selected to receive the Chairman Quality Award is a big deal. The winners of the Chairman Quality Awards are invited to Columbus, Indiana, to meet with the CEO and deliver a presentation to the Senior Executive Team about their Six Sigma project. This is a tremendous opportunity for employees to shine. As we move into 2009, Cummins Inc. is examining creative ways of using technology to provide online training for Black Belts and Green Belts worldwide.

Cummins Inc. is a corporation of complementary business units that design, manufacture, distribute and service engines and related technologies, including fuel systems, controls, air handling, filtration, emission solutions and electrical power generation systems. Headquartered in Columbus, Indiana, Cummins serves customers in more than 160 countries through its network of 550 company-owned and independent distributor facilities and more than 5,000 dealer locations.

71. Promote people from within.

The first place to look for future talent is in your current workforce. Often, internal or current employees make the best available candidates because they are already familiar with your company, its culture and daily operations. They also have existing relationships within the organization and with external vendors and suppliers.

When you promote from within, you already know what kind of employee you are getting. You know about the employee's work habits. You know what to expect. You also send a positive message to others in the organization by showing them that they can be on a long-term career path.

72. Celebrate success daily.

Everyone loves a pat on the back. Celebrate success and hard work daily. There are a million ways to say thank you: send a handwritten thank-you note or a thank-you e-mail, give away a plant, a poster, Hershey bars or gift certificates, invite an employee to lunch, make an announcement at the weekly staff meeting or in the company newsletter about a job well done, or treat your employee to a spa day or to a beer after work.

73. Encourage effective communication.

There are two parts to communication: sending a message and receiving a message. Effective communication occurs when the message is sent, received and understood. In other words, effective communication occurs when the two parties know what's going on.

Sending the message can be accomplished in a variety of ways: speaking, writing, using hand gestures or just looking at someone in a certain way. Receiving the message can also happen in a variety of ways: active listening, reading and watching. There is a difference between hearing a message and understanding the message.

Often, we hear but we don't understand. A few years ago, during the Christmas holidays, as my husband was heading out the door to the supermarket I asked him to buy some chips. When he got home, he handed me a bag of potato chips. I had wanted chocolate chips to add to my cookie dough batter. I said "chips," and he bought chips. I sent a message, he heard the message, but there was no understanding. Does that ever happen at work? Do people send messages that are misinterpreted? Sure it does! It happens all the time. Poor communication causes employee frustration and leads to

work needing to be redone. When employees don't understand what they are supposed to do, they can make mistakes.

74. Use cartoons to add humor to corporate communications.

Everyone likes to laugh. Using cartoons is an easy way to spice up your corporate communications. Just make sure that you are not breaking any copyright laws by copying cartoons you are not allowed to use. One resource for a variety of business cartoons is CartoonResource at www.cartoonresource.com, 616.719.1242.

75. Sing!

When all else fails, just sing. The waiters and waitresses at Johnny Rockets and Texas Roadhouse sing and dance to entertain the customers. Sailors, soldiers and pirates have been singing for years to pass the time and get their work done.

Many years ago, during a Six Sigma training program in Puerto Rico, a group of Johnson & Johnson Black Belts wrote a song called the SIPOC rap and delivered the song on the last day of the training program. It was definitely the highlight of the entire week.

So there you have it—75 ways to create a motivating work environment.

There are many more ways to create a motivating work environment. I just haven't heard of them yet. Use your imagination and try something new. If it doesn't work, try something else. The University of Michigan took a risk when they introduced the VOICES Web site. They weren't sure that it would work. Today they are proud of the Web site and technology, and they have been asked to share their approach with other universities. If your organization is doing something to create a more motivating work environment, let me know. I'd love to share it with my audiences.

About Regina M. Clark, CSP

Regina M. Clark is an international speaker, corporate trainer and founder of Clark Training and Development, a communication consulting firm in New York. Regina has spoken to audiences around the world about leadership, process improvement, innovation, powerful communication and having fun. Her clients include Johnson & Johnson, Paccar, Cummins, BASF and others. Regina is the author of two books, *Developing Process Excellence Leaders* and *Deadlines & Diapers: 65 Tips for Working Moms*. If you are interested in booking Regina for your next event, go to www.reginaclark.net or call 845-294-7089.

Breinigsville, PA USA
17 March 2010
234372BV00005B/7/P

9 780615 280806